Aging America Resources

Care Ministry

Biblical Caregiving

Principles & Workbook

Blessed are the Caregivers

Charles Puchta

1st. Edition

Aging America Resources Care Ministry is a division of Aging America Resources, Inc. The Care Ministry (*www.CareMinistry.com*) complements the approach of Aging America Resources by helping people understand and apply biblical principles to aging and caregiving. Aging America Resources (*www.AgingUSA.com* and *www.AgingAmericaResources.com)* is dedicated to helping families cope and care for aging loved ones. We focus on:

- Educating and informing people on the issues they are likely to encounter as loved one's age.
- Helping families realize the many wonderful organizations that are available and how to locate resources in their area.
- Providing families with practical information tools and exercises so they can apply the information to their situation.
- Showing people the big picture so they understand the issues and options.
- Explaining how issues "Interlock" so they know what to expect and avoid getting blindsided by seemingly unrelated issues.

All scripture quotations, unless otherwise indicated, are taken from the HOLY BIBLE, NEW INTERNATIONAL VERSION®. NIV®. Copyright ©1973, 1978, 1984 by International Bible Society. Used by permission of Zondervan. All rights reserved.

Scripture quotations marked (NLT) are taken from the Holy Bible, New Living Translation, copyright © 1996. Used by permission of Tyndale House Publishers, Inc., Wheaton, Illinois 60189. All rights reserved.

Greetings,

Scripture provides instruction for people taking on the role of caregiver and is a phenomenal source of purpose and inspiration. This book is dedicated to helping people understand and apply biblical caregiving principles and provides a spiritual approach to helping you help your aging loved one.

When times are tough, as they often are, I find comfort in knowing that the Lord has a plan for my life. While I have been devastated over the illness and loss of both my parents while in my thirties, I can look back now and see how God has used my experience for good.

This book complements *The Aging America Resource Guide.* Used together, I am confident families will face the many challenges with purpose and peace. Our objective in both books is to provide practical information, tools and tips that you can apply to your personal situation. There are no absolute answers. Rather, we hope to provoke thoughts and discussion through our presentation of the topics and scripture that will help you determine what is best or most appropriate for your family.

May God's peace be with you!

In Christ,

Charles Puchta

*This book is dedicated to the many wonderful people
who have been with me along my faith journey
and encouraged me along the way.*

*Special thanks to my wife Karen, sister Polly, and
brother (in-law and in Christ) Gregg.
Your support, love and belief in me have been heartfelt.
Also, to our daughters Josie, Ellie and Abbie,
even though you are only children,
your passion for the Lord and serving others
is already evident in so many ways.
If we could all have such a child-like approach to life,
the world would be a better place.*

*Thanks also to wonderful leadership at my church,
Montgomery Community Baptist Church, in Cincinnati, Ohio.
The inspiration and motivation I receive from
Sr. Pastor Tom Lipsey, Pastor Debbie Handkins,
Pastor Dick Eckhardt and Director of Care
Ministry Carla Biddle are incredible.
I am honored to call each of you a friend.*

TABLE OF CONTENTS

Section 1:
Give Me Strength

God never promised us days without pain and disappointment, laughter without sorrow and sadness, sun without rain, but He did promise strength to get through each day, comfort for the tears, and light for the way. As you provide care and support for your aging parent, spouse, relative or friend, turn to God for strength and hope.

Whether the years have finally caught up with your aging family member, or your loved one is afflicted by illness or disease, it can be a trying time for the entire family. The scriptural passages referenced throughout this book, provide wonderful guidance and instruction to families as they encounter the many challenges associated with aging and caregiving.

> *"The LORD gives strength to his people, the Lord blesses his people with peace."* – **Psalm 29:11**

Have faith. Trust God! He is in control, and He knows what you're going through. He uses all situations for good.

> *"And we know that in all things God works for the good of those who love him"* – **Romans 8:28a**

While at times we may not understand, if we seek Him with all of our heart, God promises to meet our needs and answer our prayers.

BLESSINGS

For many people our lives have become such a routine that we take things for granted. A bump in the road can be a necessary wake-up call to get us to stop and reflect on the many ways our lives are blessed each and every day. One of those blessings is our health. Often it is only when we are worn out, experience on-going pain, or end up in the hospital that we recognize the truly precious gift of good health. Unfortunately for many older people, an ailment or disease such as arthritis, bronchitis, or cancer can cause them to live in pain daily. For those of us who are generally healthy, it can be difficult to understand how an elderly or ill person feels.

As you take on the role of caregiver, a few things typically happen.
1. You become more aware of your health.
2. You come to recognize and appreciate that maintaining your own personal health is a necessity to being a caregiver
3. You become aware of your own mortality.

The mental, physical and spiritual health of the caregiver is critical. If the caregiver is not healthy, he or she will be unable to effectively serve in a care capacity.

Stop and for a minute and think of how complex the human body is and what a miracle life really is. Also think of how we use and abuse our bodies each and every day. Isn't it amazing that our bodies last as long as they do? Give thanks to the Lord for your health each and everyday. After all, your body is your earthly home and is a blessing from God. There is a lot of truth in the saying *"You can't put a price on good health."* Our health becomes a cornerstone to everything we do each day. Make sure to take steps to preserve your own health.

THE BIBLE HAS THE ANSWER!

The Bible is truly awesome! I am constantly amazed at how everything imaginable is addressed in it.

"For the word of God is living and active."- **Hebrews 4:12a**

Both the Old and New Testaments of the Bible share God's desire for us related to aging and caregiving. As you face challenges applying scripture to your role as a caregiver, it is vitally important to remember that *the Bible is not a book of suggestions.* It is a book of instruction providing truth, strength and hope. To find joy and peace, we need to turn to the Word and apply it to all facets of our lives. Scripture provides the direction and purpose to know and do what is right. Through the understanding and application of biblical principles presented in this book, we'll help you help your aging loved one.

THE FOUR INTERLOCKING CATEGORIES

Aging America Resources groups aging and caregiving issues into four categories: **Lifestyle, Emotional, Administrative, and Memorial.** We are unique in that Aging America Resources is the only resource to emphasize the interdependency or correlation between the categories.

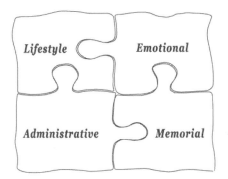

The categories and a brief description of each are as follows:

Lifestyle: Addressing a person's medical condition or diagnosis, functioning level (both physical and mental), care needs, age appropriate activities, living arrangements, driving, nutrition and more.

Administrative: Coordinating the legal and financial matters including insurance coverage – medical, life and long term care insurance; Social Security benefits including Medicare and Medicaid; financial resources such as IRA's, pension plans, savings, and other assets; Estate Planning including wills, trusts, and other legal documents of instructions such as Power of Attorney.

Emotional: Understanding your parent's perspective, coping and managing your feelings, understanding the concept of detachment, being confident in your decision making, and identifying and leveraging support resources.

Memorial: Memorializing someone's life before, during and after death, funeral considerations and preparation, preserving memories, handling of sentimental treasures, and generation planning.

For the purpose of consistency with our complementary book, *The Aging America Resource Guide*, we have grouped scripture under 10 major headings and then present it in the four categories as indicated.

1. Honor Your Father and Mother *(Lifestyle)*
2. Obey, Respect and The Golden Rule *(Lifestyle)*
3. Caregiving Instruction *(Lifestyle)*
4. Loving One Another *(Lifestyle)*
5. Sharing Thoughts and Feelings *(Emotional)*
6. Forgiveness and Reconciliation *(Emotional)*
7. Friendships and Support *(Emotional)*
8. Provisions and Needs *(Administrative)*
9. Death Considerations *(Memorial)*
10. Faith and Eternal Life *(Memorial)*

NOTE: *As you study the Bible, you will certainly find many more references to each topic discussed in this book. In selecting scripture, a concerted effort was made to include passages that have unique messages as opposed to pulling multiple passages all emphasizing the same points.*

STUDY AND APPLICATION APPROACH

The approach we suggest to helping you understand and apply scripture is summed up by the following five words:

- COLLECT
- SELECT
- INSPECT
- DISSECT
- REFLECT

COLLECT: Start by collecting yourself. Eliminate distractions and begin with prayer. Ask the Holy Spirit to open your heart and mind, and to guide you in your study and in your caregiving role.

SELECT: Many passages of scripture have been selected that are specific to aging and caregiving. While we make specific reference to a number of passages, rest assured that as you read the Bible, you will certainly find additional passages that pertain to each topic.

INSPECT: Read or inspect the entire passage so you are able to understand and apply the concept in context.

DISSECT: Look at the scripture to identify key elements, important words or ideas, repetition, tenses, etc. Aging America Resources offers our perspective on the scripture and shares thoughts and considerations.

REFLECT: At the end of each chapter, we share a number of questions for you to reflect on. Also, we encourage you to be prayerful about everything as you seek to understand your caregiver role

Regardless of whether you are using this book for a small group study, as the basis for an on-going support group, or for your personal enjoyment and application, you might find it helpful to focus on the scripture either by the ten (10) headings or four (4) categories.

Dear Heavenly Father, help me to be faithful to that which You have called me to do and help me to fully recognize that calling in my life. Help me to unselfishly repay my parents with love and support during their times of need. Help me, Lord, to honor my parent(s) in every way. Please fill me with your Spirit, Lord, so that love, gentleness, kindness and patience are ever present in my life. In Jesus' precious and holy name. Amen.

SECTION 2
Lifestyle Reflections

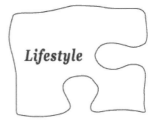

HONOR YOUR FATHER AND MOTHER

Exodus 20:12 – "Honor your father and your mother, so that you may live long in the land the LORD your God is giving you."

Deuteronomy 27:16a – "Cursed is the man who dishonors his father or his mother."

Proverbs 23:22 – "Listen to your father, who gave you life, and do not despise your mother when she is old."

Matthew 19:19 – "honor your father and mother, and love your neighbor as yourself."

* * * * * * * * *

In the second book of the Bible, we see the first reference to *'honoring our father and mother.'* In the book of Exodus we learn the 10 Commandments, the fifth of which is: *"Honor your father and mother, so that you may live long in the land the Lord your God is giving you."* Written as a Commandment, this is not a choice or suggestion. Rather it is a mandate or requirement.

IT'S ALL ABOUT HONOR

The words that stick out in the fifth commandment are: *"Honor," "so that,"* and *"live long."* Starting with the word *'Honor'*, we begin by turning to Webster's dictionary to understand the meaning. Webster's uses the words *"high respect; esteem; glory or recognition; distinction; high rank; great privilege"* to define *'Honor.'* In all cases, the word *'Honor'* is positive and privileged. We associate the word honor with people that have achieved a position of significance. For example, *"Your Honor"* when referring to a Judge. Or think about the *"Honor Roll"* at school, referring to those whose academic performance merits special recognition.

As you think of the word *'Honor'* in context with aging and caregiving, think about ways you might honor your parents. For example, when I think of honoring someone, I think of:

- A person who is the center of attention.
- A person that others want to be next to, rubbing shoulders with.
- A person that others want to talk with and learn from.
- A person that others are proud to refer to as a friend and confidant.

Do those descriptions of honor reflect your relationship with your father and mother? Or, is the relationship you have with your parents better described as insignificant or *"Out of Sight, Out of Mind."* Are your parents more of a nuisance and are you frustrated with having to deal with them? And, how many of us think of the saying *"You can pick your friends but you can't pick your family."* Well, if these comments at all reflect what you are thinking, think about this: God predestined each one us. He chose our parents, and while it may not be apparent at the time, He uses all things for good. So maybe simply reading this paragraph will give you a new perspective on life, aging and caregiving.

For many the struggle may be differentiating and drawing the line between honoring your parent and allowing them to take advantage of you. In this situation, it may be necessary to establish healthy boundaries. It is not uncommon for older adults to become isolated, especially if they live independently.   As such, frequent visits from their children may be a sole source of companionship.   If you're struggling to draw a healthy boundary between honoring your parent and maintaining your own life, nothing beats being prayerful and asking God to intervene to relieve parent's fears or loneliness or to show you the underlying issue(s) for your parent's actions.

Just after we are commanded to *"Honor,"* we are told why. It is important to note that the words *"so that"* are conditional. The fifth commandment is the first commandment with a promise. In other words, if we Honor, then we will receive. *(Stated another way, if we don't honor our parents, we will not receive.)* What God is offering is abundant life. When the Bible states that we will *"live long,"* this is not a guarantee that none of us will die prematurely if we honor our parents. While longevity is one blessing many of us may receive, I believe that real benefit is truly being able to live. To be able to live an abundant and blessed life that free from the bondage of stress and guilt that many people encounter when they take an active role in an aging loved one's life. Also, by honoring our parents we honor God by practicing our faith, and enjoy a closer, richer and more fulfilling relationship with Him.

ASSOCIATION INDICATES SIGNIFICANCE

We've all heard the cliché of being able to tell the character of a man by the company he keeps. We take the same approach to understanding the importance God places on the fifth commandment. Right along with the Commandment of honoring our parents we find the Commandments of *"Thou shalt not take the name of the Lord thy*

God in vain," "Thou shalt not kill", "Thou shalt not commit adultery," and *"Thou shalt not steal."* Have you ever noticed that seven of the 10 commandments specifically tell us things we must NOT do? The first commandment is also similar in that it states Thou shalt have **_No_** Other Gods Before Me. The only commandments that tell us what we MUST do are the fourth and fifth.

> 4. *"Remember the Sabbath day by keeping it holy"*
> 5. *"Honor your Father and your Mother"*

It amazing to think that God's Top 10 includes instruction on how we should respect and love our parents. Many people might have expected a Commandment to say something like *"Parents, Love and Cherish your Children raising them in a way that is pleasing to God."*

REPETITION REINFORCES THE POINT

Many more times throughout the Bible, the commandment of honoring our father and mother is reinforced and repeated. In the book of Deuteronomy we learn the consequences or punishment if we fail to honor our parents.

> *"Cursed is the man who dishonors his father or his mother."* **- Deuteronomy 27:16a**

The word cursed is essentially the opposite of blessed. Just as blessings are the reward for being obedient, curses are the punishment for disobedience. I believe it means that we will be apart from God and His will for us. We will suffer the consequences of our actions or inactions. Frankly, living life alone without God's blessings would be a lonely and trying experience. There is no greater curse than rebelling against God and forfeiting the gifts of abundant life, His blessings and love.

The word blessing, leads many people to think of the book "Prayer of Jabez". In this book, the author Bruce Wilkinson shares with us God's desire to pour out his blessing on us. Think about how much God loves each and every one of us. He loves us more than we will ever comprehend. His love is deep, wide and unconditional. And then, consider how disappointing and foolish it must be to dishonor our parents and be cursed.

CLARIFICATION ON HONORING

The books of Matthew and Proverbs indicate what we are to do, or not to do, when our parents age.

> *"Honor your father and mother, and love your neighbor as yourself"* - **Matthew 19:19**

> *"Listen to your father, who gave you life, and do not despise your mother when she is old."* - **Proverbs 23:22**

Most people have heard and thought about what it means to *"Love your neighbor as yourself,"* however, the Proverbs passage is less known. The idea of listening to your father suggests the idea of wisdom and experience, sort of like father knows best. Then, the second part of the passage is specific instruction telling what not to do: *"do not despise your mother when she is old."* I might have expected something more like, be patient, loving and kind with your mother as she ages. But the point is more clearly stated by taking a negative to insinuate a positive. It is, as though it is a normal reaction to get frustrated with our mother and therefore, we need to be told avoid becoming irritated or annoyed with our loved ones.

Often times as a loved ones age, it is easy to get frustrated at little things and become impatient. Our parents might not be as quick witted, or are slower in the pace, stubborn or independent. As their abilities deteriorate, our frustration increases and the slightest thing may cause us to loose our temper. We often overlook the wisdom and experience they can offer us.

A friend recently made a comment that merits mention. Too often we choose to isolate our older adults and create special groups just for them. Why not look to involve them and integrate them throughout our churches and lives. They have the time, they have the talent, and they treasure the opportunity to share with others and be recognized for their contributions. Are you recognizing the older adults in your life for their wisdom and experience or are you trying to find places to hide them and get them out of the way?

So what does all this mean? First and foremost, honoring our parents is not only the right thing to do; it is something that God has commanded us to do. As a commandment, it is important to clarify that this is not a suggestion or choice. The word Commandment connotes authority or law.

SETTING YOUR PRIORITIES

I have never met a person who has said *"I have so much free time in my life, let me know what I can do to help."* Instead what I most commonly hear is *'I'll try to squeeze you in next week,'* or *'I won't be able to get you on my schedule until next month.'* The point is that our lifestyles have most people running frantically from place to place. However, what's interesting is that people always seem to find the time to do the things they really want to do. And, the flip side is that people can always come up with lots of excuses to not do the things they don't want to do.

Are your parents a priority in your life? Do you prioritize them into your schedule or do you try to fit them in here and there? To truly honor your father and mother, they should be a priority in your life. Whether it is talking with them on the telephone a couple of times each week, seeing them in person on a regular basis, or having frequent contact with them, some level of regular contact is consistent with the expectation of honor.

If you come from what may be described as a dysfunctional family, where family relations are strained or even damaged, honoring your father and mother may be difficult to swallow, however, I have not read anything in the Bible that indicates any exceptions.

When I think of the saying *"Altitude is a reflection of Attitude,"* I think of it in a heavenly sense. That is, the better our attitude about the situations and challenges we face, the easier it is to be more Christ-like and enjoy abundant life. Jesus never turned away at the sight of lepers. He never spoke out against those who flogged and crucified him. Rather he accepted them and prayed for them. In fact, he tells us that if someone hits us on one cheek, we should turn and offer up the other. Even though for many people family relationships are anything but perfect, our responsibility remains the same.

If your family relationship is best described as challenged or non-existent, spend time in prayer asking the Lord for strength, guidance, direction and how to go about reconciliation. It seems like so often we are creatures of habit. We know how someone is going to react before a situation occurs. Maybe by surprising someone with a loving gesture they did not expect, or that catches them off-guard, you can begin to mend broken relationships and honor your parents in a way that is pleasing to God.

* * * * * * * *

Questions & Considerations for Reflection and Discussion

What does the word 'Honor' mean to you?

What are some recent examples of how you have honored your aging loved one(s)?

What are some different ways you would like to Honor your loved one in the future? Is God putting something heavy on your heart? Be specific with things you'd like to do in the next month, three-months, six months, etc.

What's one thing you might do today or this week to Honor your loved one?

As you incorporate new ways of honoring your parents in your day-to-day life, jot down the things you are going to do differently. Spend time in prayer and meditation asking for guidance, direction, healing and restoration of relationships. Then, in a month or two, look back at your list and reflect on how God has answered your prayers and how you feel about the relationship you enjoy with your parents or loved ones. Altitude is often a reflection of our attitude.

OBEY, RESPECT AND THE GOLDEN RULE

Ephesians 6:1 – "Children, obey your parents in the Lord, for this is right."

Colossians 3:20 – "Children, obey your parents in everything, for this pleases the Lord."

Leviticus 19:32 – "Rise in the presence of the aged, show respect for the elderly and revere your God. I am the LORD."

Matthew 7:12 – "So in everything, do to others what you would have them do to you, for this sums up the Law and the Prophets."

* * * * * * * * *

OBEYING

The concept of obeying our parents teaches us that we are accountable for everything that we do in life. We all make good choices and bad choices. Some that we are happy with and others that we will regret and have to suffer the consequences. All through life our parents and other authority figures have been telling us to obey and do as we are told.

"But what if I don't agree with them?" "What if they are just plain wrong?" After all, Colossians says '*obey your parents in everything*'. Does this mean that we should offer assistance and make suggestions and if they don't agree or accept our offers to participate or help that we should simply roll over and do as they request?

I believe there are a number of questions we should address in order to know what to do.

- Is your parent or loved one of sound mind and able to make an informed decision? Or, might they be acting out of fear?
- What are the risks if you do nothing and do not challenge your parent or even forcefully push your opinion?

In terms of sound judgment, let's use an analogy to demonstrate the importance of distinguishing between *"Needs"* and *"Wants."* Often older people can be in denial of what's best for them, set in their ways and be resistant to accepting assistance. Words that are often associated with Senior Citizens include *"Independent," "Prideful,"* and *"Stubborn."* As a result they may *"Want"* to do things their way and without assistance. In fact, it is not uncommon for older people to hide from their family the challenges they are facing, as they may not *"Want"* to become a burden. Recognize that change can be hard for anyone, especially an older person. So, if you believe that your parent's health indicates a *"Need"* for care, and they don't *"Want"* to accept the approach or care option you are suggesting, it might be worth taking a step back. Before you start encouraging change, try looking at the situation differently. Try to understand your parent's perspective. Put yourself in their shoes. Help them to realize the risks, danger or fallacies in their reasoning and the benefits or plusses from the alternatives.

In terms of risks, it is important to understand and give consideration to what might happen if you do not challenge your parent. For example, what if they should fall in their own home and not be able to get to a phone for help? What are the risks or possibility of them leaving the stove on and causing a fire? What if you have concerns for your parents driving and their ability to react to an unexpected situation? Here you should consider both your parents and any innocent bystanders that could be effected.

BALANCING OBEYING VS. HONORING

As parents age and become more dependent, we need to apply all the lessons we have learned throughout life and from the Bible to help us discern what is best or right for a particular situation. While we are commanded to obey our parents, we know that God has the ultimate authority over our lives and we must obey His Word.

Honoring our parents may be in conflict with obeying them. It may mean making tough decisions against their wishes. We should always keep their best interests in mind and not let our own **wants** get in the way of their **needs**. You know in your heart if your motivation is pure and honorable as you decide to intervene and make a decision directly contradicting your parent. A reminder though, God knows our thoughts and our hearts better than we do, so be honest with yourself when examining your motives.

In John 9:23 we see an example where a parent defers to a grown child to speak for himself. The passage states, *"He is of age, ask him."* Once a person reaches a certain age, they are accountable and expected to make their own decisions. If you do not believe that your parent is making rationale decisions, consider the risks of not doing anything to intervene. Where is the greater risk or danger? I don't think God wants us to allow our parents to endanger themselves or anyone around them. It may be helpful to consider the greater good. The combination of matching a person's needs with the available options is something you will want to pray about. God will impress upon you the answer and enable you to make your best-informed decision that ultimately honors and obeys your parent and Him as well.

RESPECTING OUR ELDERS

Most of us have been told to respect our elders since we were kids. What does it mean to respect our elders? It may be easier to understand the meaning and application of the word respect by first looking at the word 'disrespect'.

Disrespect includes such things as ignoring someone's thoughts or feelings, talking to them in a condescending manner, neglecting them in times of need, forcing your opinion on someone, being rude or selfish. Now consider the opposites. There seems to be a strong connection between the words Honor, Obey and Respect. I think of The Golden Rule. *"Do unto others as you would have them do to you."*- **Luke 6:31.** Isn't that really what it is all about?

The poem on the following page entitled the wooden bowl shares a story that makes the point clear.

THE WOODEN BOWL

A frail old man went to live with his son, daughter-in-law and 4-year-old grandson. The old man's hands trembled, his eyesight blurred, and his step faltered. The family ate together at the table, but the elderly grandfather's shaky hands and failing sight made eating difficult. Peas rolled off the spoon onto the floor. When he grasped the glass, milk spilled on the tablecloth. The son and daughter-in-law became irritated with the mess. "We must do something with Grandpa," said the son. "I have had enough of spilled milk, noisy eating, and food on the floor." So the husband and the wife set a small table in the corner.

There Grandpa ate alone while the rest of the family enjoyed their dinner. Since Grandpa had broken a dish or two, his food was served in a wooden bowl. When the family glanced in Grandpa's direction, sometimes he had a tear in his eye as he sat alone. Still the only words the couple had for him were sharp admonitions when he dropped his fork or spilled food. The 4 year old watched it all in silence.

One evening before supper, the father noticed his son playing with wood scraps on the floor. He asked the child sweetly, "What are you making?" Just as sweetly the boy responded, "Oh, I am making a little wooden bowl for you to eat your food when you grow old." The 4 year old smiled and went on with his work.

The words so struck the parents that they were speechless. Then tears started to stream down their cheeks. Though no words were spoken, both knew what must be done. That evening the husband took the Grandfather's hand and gently led him to the family table. For the remainder of his days he ate every meal with the family. For some reason, neither the husband nor wife seemed to care any longer when a fork dropped, milk spilled, or the tablecloth soiled.

- Author Unknown

WISDOM FROM EXPERIENCE

What's so special about our Elders? Our elders have wisdom from their life experiences. Maybe, just maybe, we might be able to learn a valuable lesson in life from them. Basically, we should treat our elders with dignity and honor. Don't sweat the small stuff and get frustrated by the little things our aging loved one's do by omission or commission. Instead, recognize the many ways that God made your parents special. Cherish the wit and wisdom and be thankful that you have a parent or loved one to enjoy. Respecting your elders is not just something your mother told you to do, it is something that God has instructed us to do.

I recall seeing a bumper sticker that puts things into perspective. It read, *"Be nice to your children because someday they may pick your nursing home."* The opportunity this points out is that showing respect to your parents is not only the right thing to do, but it also teaches your children how to properly respect older adults and eventually how to treat you.

* * * * * * * *

Questions & Considerations for Reflection and Discussion

What do the words 'Obey' and 'Respect' mean to you?

What are some examples of situations you can think of where hiding or stuffing your feelings or concerns might not be in your parent's best interest?

What are some ways you might talk to your parent differently to understand his/her concerns and also express your concerns?

Are there scenarios you might talk to your parent about now to gain an understanding of his/her perspective before a potential situation arises? *(e.g., what are characteristics of a safe driver? What are examples of things that might suggest a person's inability to live independently? etc.)*

What lessons are you directly or indirectly teaching your children about how they should treat you when you are older?

Guilt can be a burden that haunts people for years. What are ways that you can move forward with confidence knowing that you are doing the right thing (even if it is against your parent's wishes)?

CAREGIVING INSTRUCTION

1 Timothy 5:4 – "But if a widow has children or grandchildren, these should learn first of all to put their religion into practice by caring for their own family and so repaying their parents and grandparents, for this is pleasing to God."

1 Timothy 5:8 – "If anyone does not provide for his relatives, and especially for his immediate family, he has denied the faith and is worse than an unbeliever."

Galatians 6:2 – "Carry each other's burdens, and in this way you will fulfill the law of Christ."

* * * * * * * *

RESPONSIBILITY FOR CARE

In the 1st Timothy passage, God clearly indicates that taking care of our immediate family and relatives is an expectation of us that brings glory and honor to God.

> *"But if a widow has children or grandchildren, these*
> *should learn first of all to put their religion into*
> *practice by caring for their own family and so*
> *repaying their parents and grandparents, for this is*
> *pleasing to God".* - **1 Timothy 5:4**

While this passage references widows, it points out that caring is a demonstration of our faith – *"put their religion into practice by caring."* In fact, it is our responsibility to care for our own family. And, we are also told why, because repaying our parents is pleasing to God. The reference to family is not only our immediate family but also to our decedents. So, when we get married, and we leave our mother and father and become one with our husband/wife, we do not relinquish our family ties and responsibility. The repaying reference suggests that our parents have done a tremendous amount for us, and now it is our turn to give back to them. Our faith also instructs us to *"love our neighbor has ourselves"* and be selfless not selfish. Essentially, caring for our family members enables us to live our faith and please God with all that we do.

In the second passage from 1st Timothy, God clearly indicates how He feels about those that neglect their home.

"If anyone does not provide for his relatives, and especially for his immediate family, he has denied the faith and is worse than an unbeliever." - **1 Timothy 5:8**

An operative word in this passage is *"Provide."* According to Webster's the word provide means: *"To furnish; supply: provide food and shelter for a family; To make available; to set down as a stipulation; and to make ready ahead of time; prepare."* The word 'provide' is a verb indicating action is involved. In other words, we can't just sit there, we need to do something. The second part of the passages makes it clear that if we do not uphold our responsibility, we are not being faithful to God and are *"worse than an unbeliever."* It strikes me that by knowing our responsibility and failing to do what is expected of us is worse, not equivalent, to an unbeliever. Maybe an unbeliever simply doesn't know better, but, since we know, there is an expectation for us to provide care for our families. Giving back, providing care and support, and showing our love in all that we do is pleasing to God and expected.

NO DISPENSATION FOR DISTANCE

With more and more families spread out across the country or even the globe, our responsibility to our families remains the same as if we are next door. We still have a responsibility to provide care. Often times people compare young children who are dependents to older adults requiring care. As our loved ones get older, they often become more dependent on family, friends and neighbors and there can be a general inability to cope. As such, the things we might have done for our dependent children are the same kinds of things we may find ourselves needing to do for our dependent parents or grandparents.

Give some consideration to the types of things you do for your young children that maybe you should be doing for a dependant older parent. Essentially, we encourage them in many ways including:

- We reinforce the importance of eating their vegetables
- We do their laundry and change their bed linens

- We help them brush their teeth
- We help them manage their allowance
- We plan many of their daily activities

CARRYING THE BURDEN

Continuing with our analogy of children and parents, I am reminded of how the needs of our kids, for the most part, dictates the things we will do over the course of the day. For example, our daughters need to be driven to and picked up from school at specific times. If they participate in extracurricular activities or sports, we as parents have a responsibility to get them to and from activities and to enthusiastically support them at recitals, school plays and games. And, just as it may not be someone's first choice to watch a soccer game in the rain on a chilly Saturday morning or to attend out of town swim meets, we do it regardless of how burdensome it may become.

> *"Carry each other's burdens, and in this way you will fulfill the law of Christ."* - **Galatians 6:2**

The Galatians passage makes reference to carrying each other's burdens and indicates that by doing so we fulfill the law of Christ. Just as we meet our kids needs according to the schedule that is set for us, should this be any different to how we address the needs of our dependent parents?

If our child is sick and needs to go to the doctor, what parent wouldn't miss a day of work to see that he or she received the proper medical attention? Are you ready and willing to do the same for your parent? As we consider our responsibilities to care for our parents we will all face a number of choices. Know that you're not alone and you don't need to do everything on your own. Fortunately, there are many wonderful organizations and programs that can provide the level and type of care deemed appropriate for your situation. Services are available to help with everything from providing assessment and counseling services to providing care services either on a part-time or full-time basis in a variety of settings.

Just as God enables us to rise to each new occasion or challenge, He also equips us with the tools and resources needed. The focus of our complementary book, *The Aging America Resource Guide*, is to provide practical information to help people by equipping them with the tools and resources to make informed decisions and work through issues by applying the information for your particular situation.

As we mentioned earlier in this section, who among us will not make the time for the things that are truly important to us. Gods tells us clearly that our family and home should be priorities.

* * * * * * * *

Questions & Considerations for Reflection and Discussion

What do the words 'Provide' and 'Care' mean to you? What are specific examples of how you might care for your aging loved one in a manner that would be pleasing to God?

What are some of the things that tend to divert you from your responsibility to your family?

What are some ways you might handle or prioritize things differently so as to care for your parent?

What are some sacrifices you need to make in your day-to-day life to honor God, yourself, and your parents?

How might making sacrifices send a clear message to your children of what is important and what is expected? What might some of the benefits be?

While making sacrifices may not be easy, these are instructions from God. Know that God will give you the strength, and the wisdom to help you carry out His will. Spend time in prayer asking God for direction and encouragement so that you can fulfill your family responsibilities.

LOVING ONE ANOTHER

1 John 3:11 – "This is the message you heard from the beginning: We should love one another."

1 John 3:16 & 18 – "This is how we know what love is: Jesus Christ laid down his life for us. And we ought to lay down our lives for our brothers. [18]Dear children, let us not love with words or tongue but with actions and in truth."

1 Corinthians 13:4-8a – "Love is patient, love is kind. It does not envy, it does not boast, it is not proud. It is not rude, it is not self-seeking, it is not easily angered, it keeps no record of wrongs. Love does not delight in evil but rejoices with the truth. It always protects, always trusts, always hopes, always perseveres. Love never fails."

* * * * * * * *

Three of the most powerful words in the English language are the words *"I LOVE YOU."* The scripture from 1st John states that God expects us to love one another. In fact, in the book of Matthew, He even tells us to love and pray for our enemies. He also tells us how we should love.

> *"Dear children, let us not love with words or tongue but with actions and in truth."* – **1 John 3:18**

We see that love includes what comes from our heart, mouth, and body. Also, the reference to truth suggests that to truly experience love we must be honest with others and ourselves.

NO STONE LEFT UNTURNED

When I think of love, I think of how I love my children. I think of my role as a loving father in terms of teacher, coach, encourager and defender. I think of sharing in their joy, pain and disappointment. Is that how you think of love when you think of your parents?

The Corinthians passage defines the elements of Love.
- *Love* is patient
- *Love* is kind
- *Love* does not envy
- *Love* is not proud
- *Love* is not rude
- *Love* is not self-seeking
- *Love* is not easily angered
- *Love* keeps no record of wrongs
- *Love* does not delight in evil but rejoices with the truth
- *Love* always protects, always trusts, always hopes, and always perseveres
- *Love* never fails

It strikes me that the difference between the words Live and Love is one letter – I. So often the thing that can be holding someone back from loving and living is the 'I'. That is the person that stares back at you from the mirror. If instead of I, you said O, think of the symbols that represent hugs and kisses as XXXOOO. Maybe it's time to love and live more? Is there anything holding you back?

DON'T TAKE LOVE FOR GRANTED

One of the things I often hear is that family members don't directly say the words "I LOVE YOU." Instead, they often say things in a round about way such as *"You know I love you."* Also, the words "I love you" can often be diluted as they are said more as a salutation. In other words, instead of saying 'Goodbye,' many people have come to substitute the words 'I love you.' If you haven't shared an honest to goodness heartfelt I LOVE YOU recently, try holding someone's hand, looking him or her straight in the eyes and deliberately say "I love you." Unfortunately, I have heard many people wish they said I love you one last time, or they may question if a loved one really knew in his or her heart how much they loved and appreciate them. Our point is simply don't assume or take love for granted. Say it! Mean it! And, as the 1 John 3:18 passage indicates, our actions and truth are essential.

* * * * * * * *

Questions & Considerations for Reflection and Discussion

How does the definition of love in the Corinthians passage relate to your relationship with your aging loved ones?

When was the last time you told your parent(s) that you love them?

What are some ways that you might show and express your love in a more heartfelt way?

What might be some barriers to loving someone from the bottom of your heart?

Spend some time considering God's agape love for you and what makes that love so special.

 Dear Lord of heaven and earth, when circumstances cause me to feel overwhelmed, help me to remember that You are my refuge. I trust in You and know that You use all situations for good. Your word and Your promises give me strength when I am weak. May Your Holy Spirit fill my heart and guide me one day at a time. I love You with all of my heart and I thank You for your unwavering love. In Jesus' name. Amen.

SECTION 3
Emotional Considerations

Emotional

SHARING THOUGHTS AND FEELINGS

Proverbs 16:24 – "Pleasant words are a honeycomb, sweet to the soul and healing to the bones."

Job 6:24-25 – "Teach me, and I will be quiet; show me where I have been wrong. How painful are honest words! But what do your arguments prove?"

Ephesians 4:15 – "Instead, speaking the truth in love, we will in all things grow up into him who is the Head, that is, Christ."

Galatians 5:22-26 – "But the fruit of the Spirit is love, joy, peace, patience, kindness, goodness, faithfulness, gentleness and self-control. Against such things there is no law. Those who belong to Christ Jesus have crucified the sinful nature with its passions and desires. Since we live by the Spirit, let us keep in step with the Spirit. Let us not become conceited, provoking and envying each other."

* * * * * * * * *

Express Yourself

All too often when faced with a stressful situation, people don't communicate their thoughts well. They later have regrets, which can be something they didn't say that they wish they had, or something they did say that they wish they hadn't. When expressing yourself to family members, be careful to:

Say What You Mean,
Mean What You Say.
Just Don't Say It Mean!

The Proverbs passage addresses two key elements, the heart and the bones.

"Pleasant words are a honeycomb, sweet to the soul and healing to the bones." - **Proverbs 16:24**

Pleasant words are sweet to the soul, or in other words are heartfelt. I believe that it is our hearts that help us to smile brighter, hug tighter, and live lighter *(free from the bondage of our sin.)* Then we're told that pleasant words are in fact healing to our bones. I think of bones as an infrastructure. As such, if one part of the infrastructure were fragile, frail or flawed, how easy it would be for the whole body to fail. Pleasant words are basically said to be good medicine. While it can be so easy to find fault in almost everything, the real challenge can be looking for the good in everything. God is a perfect example. He knows we are sinners down to the very core of our being, yet, He loves us and lifts us up. Don't take the negative or the *"my glass is half empty"* approach. Instead, share kind words, look for the good in everything and live a life better represented by the *"my glass is half full"* attitude.

VARIETY – THE SPICE OF LIFE

Just as women are from Venus and men are from Mars, birth order and so many other things can have an impact on personalities, styles, and the things we say and do. While some people think, *"if everyone thought as I did, the world would be a much better place,"* the fact is that we are all different by God's design. In the Job passage, the first two words are *"Teach me,"* not *"Loose patience with me,"* or *"Scream at me and leave the room in a huff"*, or *"Give up on me."* No, the words are *"Teach me."* We all see things differently and talking to someone with a different perspective, point-of-view or personality can help us understand things that we wouldn't otherwise recognize. We've all heard the saying *"You're too close to the forest to see the trees."* So often, people don't see the obvious and simply need a little bit of explanation.

> *"Teach me, and I will be quiet; show me where I have been wrong. How painful are honest words! But what do your arguments prove?"* - **Job 6:24-25**

The Job passage tells us to *"teach"* and *"show"* if we believe that someone has been wrong. Notice that it doesn't say *"rub in the other guys face,"* or *"have a chip on your shoulder for being so smart."* Then, we are alerted to the fact that honest words can be painful, as if we are being warned that we need to be careful. It is not always easy to be shown where you're wrong, *(if you don't believe me just ask my sister – ha, ha)* it can even tend to hurt. Unfortunately many people, even if they know they are wrong, may choose to defend their position, rather than give in and admit they made a mistake. Keep these things in mind. The passage also reminds us that arguments don't prove anything. In fact, arguments often show our immaturity and our inability to cope in life. Family dynamics can be quite challenging. Are you the one in the family who is outspoken? Maybe it's time to give someone else a chance to talk. Are you the one who tends to be more reserved or withdrawn? Plan your words carefully. While your words might be few, they can still be powerful.

WHAT DID YOU MEAN BY THAT?

So often people use everyday words to describe or explain something, however, other family members might hear the same words and interpret things differently. For example, close your eyes and think of the color blue. Now ask others in your family to describe in detail the color blue they were thinking of. If you're like most families, the blues were not the same. The point here is that if you're having an argument or disagreement about an issue related to aging or caregiving, don't simply assume that others are out to get you. It could be a simple difference in communication styles.

Often time's families are faced with making difficult decisions on short notice. The stress from the short time frame can be tremendous. Now, introduce family dynamics and brace yourself. At all costs, try and stay away from arguments. These are times when families need to unite for the benefit and well being of an aging loved one, not the time to tear families apart and burden loved ones with arguments.

> *"Instead, speaking the truth in love, we will in all things grow up into him who is the Head, that is, Christ."* - **Ephesians 4:15**

As the Ephesians passage says, *"speak the truth in love."* The truth can really set you free. Speak with a certain calmness about you, sharing and explaining what you're thinking, what you're suggesting and why. Simply talk and give each other turns to paraphrase and ask questions as necessary. Be careful not to exaggerate or get overly emotional.

Also, remember the scripture says how painful are honest words. It doesn't say avoid honest words because they can be painful. As such, don't put off the tough discussions for another day, instead talk in a manner that is consistent with The Golden Rule. Many times we find that once families are able to express themselves in a clear and concise manner, they can then begin to work towards a solution. *(And, often much more quickly than they might have expected.)* Words that are honest and said tactfully, even though painful, can be the first step in working toward a solution.

Remember, people don't read each other's minds. Therefore, if you don't express yourself, don't expect anyone else to know what you're thinking.

The Job passage also makes mention of being *"quiet."* God gave us each two ears and one mouth. Are you listening twice as much as you're speaking? When talking, it can be very difficult to learn. As you face challenges, remember that as long as issues are avoided, others tend to build up resentment and get further entrenched in their position and beliefs. Much of this can be avoided just by talking.

If your family is struggling with conflict and disagreement, spend time in prayer before engaging in any discussion. Ask the Lord to help everyone deal with the issues at hand in fairness and truth. Pray that the more out-spoken members of the family will take their turns listening and pray that the Lord with help the quieter one's have the courage to speak up and share their thoughts. More than anything, pray that the Lord will help you realize the ultimate goal is not who wins and loses, rather, what is best and necessary for the loved one for which everyone is concerned. Lay your burdens at the foot of the cross and ask God to open minds and soften hearts, as He impresses upon everyone His wishes and will.

SET REASONABLE EXPECTATIONS
When you are all gathered together, it might not be necessary to make a decision today. Instead, just understanding what everyone is thinking might be best. (*The Aging America Resource Guide offers a number of tools designed to help with family dynamics, discussions and decisions.*)

Remember, you can't change anyone else. The only person you can change is you. I recently received an e-mail that offers some great advice. The e-mail shares the following:

I'VE LEARNED...

- That being kind is more important than being right.
- That I can always pray for someone when I don't have the strength to help him in some other way.
- That sometimes all a person needs is a hand to hold and a heart to understand.
- That under everyone's hard shell is someone who wants to be appreciated and loved.
- That the Lord didn't do it all in one day. What makes me think I can?
- That to ignore the facts does not change the facts.
- That I can't choose how I feel, but I can choose what I do about it.

DELICATE FRUIT

The Galatians passage points out that when we are filled with the Holy Spirit, we receive the gifts of love, joy, peace, patience, kindness, goodness, faithfulness, gentleness and self-control.

> *"But the fruit of the Spirit is love, joy, peace, patience, kindness, goodness, faithfulness, gentleness and self-control."* - **Galatians 5:22**

These gifts are just what we need when sharing our thoughts and feelings. Also, take heed to the warning, *"Let us not become conceited, provoking and envying each other."* Another passage that reinforces the delicate approach we should take with others is:

> *"Do to others, as you would have them do to you."* –
> **Luke 6:31**

* * * * * * * *

Questions & Considerations for Reflection and Discussion

What would be a likely response if you opened a family discussion with prayer? What would be some of the things you might pray for?

Who might you want to share some honest words with in your family? What are things that might a conversation difficult? How might you approach the conversation?

So often perceptions can haunt us. What would be something you'd like to share or clarify with your family about yourself?

FORGIVENESS AND RECONSILIATION

Mark 11:25 – "And when you stand praying, if you hold anything against anyone, forgive him, so that your Father in heaven may forgive you your sins."

Ephesians 4:32 – "Be kind and compassionate to one another, forgiving each other, just as in Christ God forgave you."

1 Peter 4:8 – "Above all, love each other deeply, because love covers over a multitude of sins."

1 John 3:15 – "Anyone who hates his brother is a murderer, and you know that no murderer has eternal life in him."

Psalms 34:14 – "Turn from evil and do good; seek peace and pursue it."

* * * * * * * * *

GOD'S FORGIVENESS

Just as *"I Love You"* are three of the most powerful words, the words *"I'm Sorry"* can be some of the most difficult words to say. So often we'd rather forget than forgive. However, forgetting rarely works. Things said or done that have been painful for someone can often be embedded in the heart.

Each and every day, we sin. However, Jesus is our model for forgiveness. Think of the song Amazing Grace and how God *"saved a wretch like me."* We are all sinners regardless of our specific sins. What's totally awesome is that God sent his Son, Jesus Christ to pay the ultimate price. Through His grace and mercy, He forgives us of all our sins.

> *"If we confess our sins, he is faithful and just and will forgive us our sins and purify us from all unrighteousness."* - **1 John 1:9**

In fact, when God forgives, he wipes the slate clean. When you have conflict with someone, do you wipe the slate clean once there has been an apology or a request for forgiveness? Chances are that we forgive, but we never really forget. Forgetting can be difficult, however it is the Christ-like thing to do. If we truly forgive, we should treat others as if something that was offensive to us never took place. It is important when a similar situation occurs in the future not to react based on memories, but to act based on biblical principles. Also, if you are struggling to forgive someone, how can you expect God to forgive you?

LOOK AHEAD

If you spend your time looking in the rearview mirror to see what's behind you, sooner or later, you're going to crash. It's just a matter of time. Instead, I believe that God wants us to live for today.

> *"But seek first his kingdom and his righteousness, and all these things will be given to you as well. Therefore do not worry about tomorrow, for tomorrow will worry about itself. Each day has enough trouble of its own."* – **Matthew 6:33-34**

Put the circumstances of your past behind you and get on with the wonderful plan God has in store for you. We all have certain regrets. Thankfully God forgives us. Maybe it's now time for you to truly forgive yourself? Stop beating yourself up for bad choices of the past, and move forward.

BEING KIND

Sometimes, we are so wrapped up in our own life that we simply tune out others. The Ephesians passage tells us to be both kind and compassionate.

> *"Be kind and compassionate to one another, forgiving each other, just as in Christ God forgave you."* - **Ephesians 4:32**

In fact, I'm not sure that either can stand alone. I think that being kind reflects how we act or react toward others. In essence, it has to do with how we treat others. Are you putting the needs of others before yourself? Is the word that best describes you SelfISH or SelfLESS?

If family dynamics have been a challenge in the past, let kindness prevail from this day forward and take whatever step are necessary to mend family relationships. Often, the tone of our voice or our approach can be our own worst enemy. If you struggle to convey your thoughts, instead of using the word 'YOU', think of how you can use the word 'I' when working through family issues. For example, instead of saying "YOU hurt me years ago when…," change your words around. Instead try "I have felt hurt since our disagreement years ago. I have had a hard time understanding why…" The simple point is that someone else can't hurt our feelings. Instead, the way we interpret someone else actions or words lead us to feel hurt. Essentially it is our reaction to a situation. For example, when our daughter's squabble, I often hear one of them playing the blame game. Wrong! Take ownership for your own feeling and actions.

ACTIONS VERSUS REACTIONS

The other passages referenced at the beginning of this section all have one thing in common. They all point out our personal responsibility. In 1st Peter we are told that *"Above all,"* we must *"love each other deeply."* Why? Because it covers a multitude of sins. Then in 1st John, we are told that if we hate our brother, we are living against God's word. In Psalms, we are being told to turn from evil and do good. Notice how it doesn't say tell your sibling or relative to turn from evil. Rather it implies that the onus is on us. We're also told to be peacemakers, which in Matthew 5 is a beatitude, and to *"seek peace and pursue it."* All of these passages refer to our personal responsibility regardless of the past.

So what happens if you make efforts to make amends and forgive others and they don't respond? Ask yourself if you've tried in a Christ-like manner to mend the relationship. If so, don't worry about their reaction. Focus on doing what is right. Also, just as God's grace and mercy is not a one-time thing, your actions and words should be consistent over time and not simply a one-time effort. Let your life reflect the loving, kind and caring character that God shows us each and every day.

GET IT OUT/DELETE IT!

Let me quickly share a strategy that works well for me. Sometimes when I get really angry with someone or something, I sit down at my computer and simply write a letter. What's unique about this approach is that I never intend to send the letter to the person who has frustrated me. Rather, I simply want to get all the negative stuff out of my mind and body, and on to paper. Then once I'm done, I simply destroy the letter and go on with my life. Matthew 8:28-34 tells us of Jesus driving out the demons from two possessed men. He sent the demons to the herd of pigs who were then destroyed by drowning. The point, get it out, don't try to cover it up.

* * * * * * * * *

Questions & Considerations for Reflection and Discussion

What events from your past are you finding challenging to let go of? Who might you want to make amends with? What are some ways you might want to express yourself that might be most effective?

What are a few random acts of kindness that you can demonstrate today, tomorrow, next week, next month, etc.? What are things that you can do pursue peace on a day-to-day basis?

What are a few ways you can demonstrate your love for others when making amends?

Is there is a situation or a person that seems rather hopeless as the damage may be too deep? What might you do? Who might you engage for help and advice?

FRIENDSHIP AND SUPPORT

Proverbs 12:15 – "The way of a fool seems right to him, but a wise man listens to advice."

Ecclesiastes 4:9-12 – "Two are better than one, because they have a good return for their work: If one falls down, his friend can help him up. But pity the man who falls and has no one to help him up! Also, if two lie down together, they will keep warm. But how can one keep warm alone? Though one may be overpowered, two can defend themselves. A cord of three strands is not quickly broken."

Galatians 6:2 – "Carry each other's burdens, and in this way you will fulfill the law of Christ."

Galatians 6:9-10 – "Let us not become weary in doing good, for at the proper time we will reap a harvest if we do not give up. Therefore, as we have opportunity, let us do good to all people, especially to those who belong to the family of believers."

Ephesians 3:16-19 – "I pray that out of his glorious riches he may strengthen you with power through his Spirit in your inner being, so that Christ may dwell in your hearts through faith. And I pray that you, being rooted and established in love, may have power, together with all the saints, to grasp how wide and long and high and deep is the love of Christ, and to know this love that surpasses knowledge - that you may be filled to the measure of all the fullness of God."

Job 34:4 – "Let us discern for ourselves what is right; let us learn together what is good."

* * * * * * * *

Just as Jesus closely surrounded himself with 12 disciples, there are numerous passages that demonstrate the importance of friends.

ADVICE AND COUNSEL

In the Proverbs passage we're told that we don't and won't ever know any better unless we seek the advice of others.

> *"The way of a fool seems right to him, but a wise man listens to advice."* - **Proverbs 12:15**

I think of the saying *"Two minds are better than one."* The point is that we are not meant to live life alone and rely solely on ourselves.

When I think of seeking advice, I think of people who have greater knowledge and wisdom than myself. To me this suggests seeking out others who have already faced similar challenges associated with aging and caregiving. Let them share their wisdom and experiences for your good.

> *"Two are better than one, because they have a good return for their work: If one falls down, his friend can help him up. But pity the man who falls and has no one to help him up! Also, if two lie down together, they will keep warm. But how can one keep warm alone? Though one may be overpowered, two can defend themselves. A cord of three strands is not quickly broken."* - **Ecclesiastes 4:9-12**

In Ecclesiastes, the concept is two are better than one. We learn the importance of having a support network. Chances are, somewhere along your journey as a caregiver, you're going to fall down. The Bible offers pity, as if you should have known better, if you do not have a support network, friend or sponsor that can help you through difficult times. My favorite is *"A cord of three strands is not quickly broken."* This refers to us, another person and God. Essentially, if we have our faith and a friend to help us through difficult times, it would take a lot to break you. The power of friendship with our brothers and sisters in Christ is amazing!

"For where two or three come together in my name, there am I with them." – **Matthew 18:20**

God often reveals himself to us through our friends. He sends our friends to us as much for comfort as for advice. Think of the following passages:

> *"A friend loves at all times, and a brother is born for adversity."* – **Proverbs 17:17**

> *"I command you to love each other in the same way that I love you. And here is how to measure it--the greatest love is shown when people lay down their lives for their friends."* – **John 15:12-13 (NLT)**

Basically, a friend in need is a friend in deed. We need friends to survive and thrive in life. I recently saw a video vignette that demonstrates the importance of friends. The video was from Nicky Gumble's Alpha course and had to do with a piece of coal. The rather profound example indicated that when a lit coal is separated from others, it would soon extinguish itself. However, once placed back with the others, it soon starts burning again. Basically, we all need friends to keep us going. The encouragement of friends can be critical, especially as new caregiving challenges unexpectedly emerge.

* * * * * * * * *

Questions & Considerations for Reflection and Discussion

Who are people that you might turn to and benefit from their wisdom and experience?

What are two or three challenges that you're currently struggling with that you might like to discuss with another person?

Who might you make aware of your current situation, to ask for prayers and support? Have you contacted your church leadership and asked for direction and advice?

When you think of ways God has blessed your life, do you think of people that are special to you? When you're facing a challenge, turn to these people for strength and hope.

Lord God, help me to become more like You in my relationships with my family members. During these difficult times, help me to remember that everyone is trying to help and do what is best. Lord, I pray that You will fill me with an extra measure of your Spirit to guide me. When I am in disagreement with someone, help me not to respond in anger, selfishness, arrogance, or pride, but in humility, understanding that it is your Will that will prevail. Help me Lord to have a servant's attitude and be loving and kind in all that I do. Lord, I pray that through our differences, we come together as a family in our faith and our love. In Jesus' name. Amen.

SECTION 4
Administrative Applications

Administrative

PROVISIONS AND NEEDS

2 Corinthians 12:14b – "After all, children should not have to save up for their parents, but parents for their children."

1 John 3:17 – "If anyone has material possessions and sees his brother in need but has no pity on him, how can the love of God be in him?"

Matthew 6:19a – "Do not store up for yourselves treasures on earth,"

Matthew 6:27 – "Who of you by worrying can add a single hour to his life?"

Matthew 6:34 – "Therefore do not worry about tomorrow, for tomorrow will worry about itself. Each day has enough trouble of its own."

Proverbs 19:20 – "Listen to advice and accept instruction, and in the end you will be wise."

Proverbs 20:18a – "Make plans by seeking advice;"

* * * * * * * * *

ROLES AND RESPONSIBILITIES

The Bible shares with us our roles, responsibilities and expectations in terms of the administrative matters.

> *"After all, children should not have to save up for their parents, but parents for their children."* - **2 Corinthians 12:14b**

The operative word from the 2nd Corinthians passage is *"should."* Should is a directional word, not a definitive word. In other words, the passage doesn't say *'do not save'* for your parents. The passage states that parents *'should'* save for their children. Unfortunately, in this day and age, many older people simply have not saved enough money to retire *'comfortably.'* And, many of those that have saved, did not expect the economy to take a turn for the worse. So while this passage suggests that ideally it won't be necessary for children to save for their parents, that may be a responsibility we face.

> *"If anyone has material possessions and sees his brother in need but has no pity on him, how can the love of God be in him?"* - **1 John 3:17**

God tells us it is our responsibility to help those in need. Furthermore, as believers, our Christ-like nature should have us offering assistance.

TREASURERS VERSUS TRUST

While the reference in 2nd Corinthians speaks of inheritance, the book of Matthew tells us that we are not to store up our treasures on earth.

Matthew suggests that it is not necessary to lavish inheritance upon of kids.

So how do we know if our parent or loved one has enough? The first tough question is how much is enough? Providing care and covering health related expenses can be quite costly. To understand and plan for the future, one recommendation is to do the planning with the help of a reputable and professional financial or estate planner. In Proverbs we are told of the importance of listening to advice and seeking advice.

> *"Listen to advice and accept instruction, and in the end you will be wise."* - **Proverbs 19:20**

> *"Make plans by seeking advice."* - **Proverbs 20:18a**

In Proverbs 19:20, the word *"Wise"* sticks out. To put the word in perspective I think of the Psalty songs for children where they sing, *"a wise man build his house upon the Rock, a foolish man builds his house upon the sand."* Based on this example, it would appear the only choice is to be wise.

While the Matthew verses tell us not to worry about tomorrow, there is a clear difference between worrying about tomorrow and planning for future life events. So, if you plan to retire at the age of 65, it would appear to be logical and consistent with biblical teachings to *"Listen to advice,"* *"accept instruction,"* and *"Make plans."*

In addition to professional advice, prayer is also critical. Ask God for guidance. Take time to understand the challenges you are likely to face as a loved one ages. Getting an idea of the various care options and costs would appear to be wise planning. That way you are able to make sound and responsible decisions either with or for your aging loved one when necessary.

* * * * * * * *

Questions & Considerations for Reflection and Discussion

Are you aware of your loved one's wishes and expectations as you serve as a caregiver? What might you want to get clarifications on?

Does your parent appear to have adequate financial resources to meet their future care needs? What might your role be?

What makes it difficult for you to focus on today versus worry about tomorrow? What are some things you might do differently?

What are some ways that you are applying the passages from Matthew 6 to your life?

Lord, You are my rock and You never fail me. Regardless of the struggles, situations, and challenges I face with my aging loved one, I am comforted to know that You are with me. Help me to turn to You when I receive troubling news, rather than feeling anger or despair. In times of sorrow and sadness, help me to put my trust and faith in You, rather than feeling hopeless. You are a sovereign God and regardless of the circumstances I know that You will use every situation for good. Lord, please comfort me and hold me in the palm of your hand during these difficult times. Lord, guide me and direct me in all that I do. In Jesus' name. Amen.

SECTION 5
Memorial Deliberations

Memorial

DEATH CONSIDERATIONS

Ecclesiastes 7:2-4 (NLT) "It is better to spend your time at funerals than at festivals. For you are going to die, and you should think about it while there is still time. Sorrow is better than laughter, for sadness has a refining influence on us. A wise person thinks much about death, while the fool thinks only about having a good time now."

2 Peter 1:15 – "And I will make every effort to see that after my departure you will always be able to remember these things."

Ecclesiastes 3:20 – "All go to the same place; all come from dust, and to dust all return."

Deuteronomy 34:5-6 – "And Moses the servant of the LORD died there in Moab, as the LORD had said. He buried him in Moab, in the valley opposite Beth Peor, but to this day no one knows where his grave is."

* * * * * * * * *

Death is a fact of life that everyone will deal with at one time or another. Death is not a taboo subject that we should avoid. While it may sound unusual, the Bible suggests we think about our own death.

GIVE PROPER CONSIDERATION

When thinking about death, spend time in preparation and give consideration to those it will impact most. As believers, we should be comforted to know we are going to a much better place. Once God says our work here is finished and calls us home, we will rejoice in the fact that for eternity, we will be with our Lord. The verses from Ecclesiastes make it clear that we should be giving consideration to issues directly related to aging and death.

> *"It is better to spend your time at funerals than at festivals. For you are going to die, and you should think about it while there is still time. Sorrow is better than laughter, for sadness has a refining influence on us. A wise person thinks much about death, while the fool thinks only about having a good time now."* - **Ecclesiastes 7:2-4 (NLT)**

Again we see reference to a wise person and are told that it is wise to think about death. We're even told that if all we do is think about having a good time now, we're foolish. Unfortunately, many people think about having a good time now simply because they don't know what to do, who to call, or how to help. Most people tend to avoid things that are difficult rather than facing them head on. However, unless you have already experienced the death of someone close to you, dealing with aging and death will be a new experience with a lot of uncertainty. This passage instructs us to use our time wisely, to prepare for and give consideration to issues related to death. Making the choice to think about somber issues such as aging and death can be difficult, especially if there are 'festivals' or other exciting things we can focus on. Sorrow helps us spend time reflecting on life and death issues and thinking of ways be can live a more abundant life and serve God.

LIVING LEGACY

Jesus left us the ultimate legacy - His Word. As we spend time in his word, we are reminded of His character, His teachings and our purpose.

> *"And I will make every effort to see that after my departure you will always be able to remember these things."* - **2 Peter 1:15**

Jesus left His legacy. Have you given much thought to your or your parent's legacy? How will your loved one be remembered? Just as Jesus planned for His departure, give some consideration to legacies within your family. What are you and your parents going to leave behind for the benefit of others? If you're uncertain about your legacy, there's no time like the present to begin creating one that you'd be happy to have live on long after you're gone.

A great way to plan ahead is to write your own obituary and epitaph. What are the focal points: Your success or your significance? Your personality or your purpose? Planning ahead can be a wonderful learning experience and a time to share in fond memories. Often times all that is left of relatives are a few pictures and select memories, which over time fade away.

HEART OF THE MATTER

All of us will eventually need to decide what is the preferred method to dispose of the dead body. As we discuss these issues, it is important to remember that God cares more about our eternal souls, than our temporary housing. Making a decision for cremation or burial is not a biblical decision, rather it is a personal preference. Depending on your up bringing and experiences, this may not be a choice for you. There may be only one option. That's fine. In fact, for many people the decision may even be based on the costs. A burial tends to be more expensive as there are a number of additional expenses that are not associated with cremation.

The following two passages reference disposition of the dead. The first addresses cremation and the second burial.

> *"All go to the same place; all come from dust, and to dust all return.* - **Ecclesiastes 3:20**

> *"And Moses the servant of the LORD died there in Moab, as the LORD had said. He buried him in Moab, in the valley opposite Beth Peor, but to this day no one knows where his grave is."*- **Deuteronomy 34:5-6**

While making the decision on how to handle a body upon death can be difficult for many, when God calls us home, the real question is going to be about your faith.

When thinking about death and funerals, people often think of last rites and paying of last respects. While the funeral is clearly a time to recognize someone's life, it is just as much for the family in terms of the grieving and closure process. When we are faced with death, we become more aware of our own mortality and give consideration to our own destiny. Whenever possible, I suggest that a funeral should be a time of celebration.

* * * * * * * * *

Questions & Considerations for Reflection and Discussion

Have you spent adequate time preparing for and giving consideration to the death of your parents or loved ones? What are a few things you might give consideration to over the coming weeks and months?

Have you given consideration to and planned for your own death? What are some things you might consider doing?

What are the legacies your loved ones will be remembered by once they are gone?

What are three or four key points that some up your life and that will be left as your legacy?

Are you aware of your loved ones wishes in terms of the disposition of their body? Are their wishes consistent with yours? Does that present any challenges you'd like to share?

FAITH AND ETERNAL LIFE

2 Corinthians 4:13-18 – "It is written: "I believed; therefore I have spoken." With that same spirit of faith we also believe and therefore speak, because we know that the one who raised the Lord Jesus from the dead will also raise us with Jesus and present us with you in his presence. All this is for your benefit, so that the grace that is reaching more and more people may cause thanksgiving to overflow to the glory of God. Therefore we do not lose heart. Though outwardly we are wasting away, yet inwardly we are being renewed day by day. For our light and momentary troubles are achieving for us an eternal glory that far outweighs them all. So we fix our eyes not on what is seen, but on what is unseen. For what is seen is temporary, but what is unseen is eternal."

John 3:16 – "For God so loved the world that he gave his one and only Son, that whoever believes in him shall not perish but have eternal life."

John 14:6 – "Jesus answered, I am the way and the truth and the life. No one comes to the Father except through me."

John 3:36 – "Whoever believes in the Son has eternal life, but whoever rejects the Son will not see life, for God's wrath remains on him."

Luke 10:25-28 – "On one occasion an expert in the law stood up to test Jesus. "Teacher," he asked, "what must I do to inherit eternal life?" "What is written in the Law?" he replied. "How do you read it?" He answered: " 'Love the Lord your God with all your heart and with all your soul and with all your strength and with all your mind; and, 'Love your neighbor as yourself." "You have answered correctly," Jesus replied. "Do this and you will live."

* * * * * * * * *

The real issue in our lives is what is the disposition of someone's soul. While we know that our salvation is based on faith and not works, do you know if your loved one has accepted Jesus into his/her heart? Does your aging family member have a personal relationship with Jesus Christ? I have heard many people express an uncertainty about their loved ones final destiny. As such, I simply say, don't assume they are saved because they go to church. Share your faith in a gentle and loving way, and ask about their relationship with Christ Jesus. If you aren't certain that your loved one is saved, share the gospel and offer to lead them in a prayer of salvation. Profess your faith and encourage your loved one to accept Christ with you now. Timing matters, don't miss the opportunity! When we come before

God, we can be certain that He will know how many people we shared the Gospel with. Don't let a loved one miss out on the wonderful eternal life and that God offers us.

Likewise, if you have a certainty about your loved one's salvation, glorify God and give thanks for the promise of eternal life and find comfort in the fact that you will once again be with your loved ones in heaven.

* * * * * * * * *

Questions & Considerations for Reflection and Discussion

What indications are there that your loved one is a believer and is saved?

What concerns do you have about the salvation of your loved one? What are some ways you might express your concerns?

List the names of five people you'd like to share the Gospel with over the course of the next few months.

Lord God, thank you so much for your majesty and sovereignty. Thank you for your incredible words to guide us along our caregiving journey as we honor the family members and friends we have the privilege of serving. Help us Lord to turn to You for strength and understanding as we face each new challenge. Help us to be a model for our children as we come to realize the very same principles you have shared with us, will some day apply to us, as we are cared for. Grant us peace as we face the realities of aging and death. And most of all Lord, encourage us to share our saving faith and have comfort that our loved ones are being called home to enjoy the splendor that awaits us with You in heaven. In Jesus' name, and for His sake. Amen.

Thanks for your Support!

Please help us to share God's strength, hope and purpose specific to the issues of aging and caregiving. As you think of others that might benefit from the Aging America Resources Care Ministry and this book please share our contact information. You might also share our ministry with the leadership at your church and suggest our resources be used for a small group study or support group.

Aging America Resources Care Ministry
www.CareMinistry.com
www.AgingUSA.com
513.205.5000